EMMANUEL JOSEPH

The Power Equation, Where Politics, Society, and Business Collide

Copyright © 2025 by Emmanuel Joseph

All rights reserved. No part of this publication may be reproduced, stored or transmitted in any form or by any means, electronic, mechanical, photocopying, recording, scanning, or otherwise without written permission from the publisher. It is illegal to copy this book, post it to a website, or distribute it by any other means without permission.

First edition

This book was professionally typeset on Reedsy.
Find out more at reedsy.com

Contents

1	Chapter 1: The Origins of Power	1
2	Chapter 2: The Interplay of Politics and Power	3
3	Chapter 3: The Role of Society in Power Dynamics	5
4	Chapter 4: Economic Power and Business Influence	7
5	Chapter 5: Globalization and the Shifting Power Dynamics	9
6	Chapter 6: Technology and the Future of Power	11
7	Chapter 7: The Intersection of Business and Politics	13
8	Chapter 8: The Role of Media in Power Dynamics	15
9	Chapter 9: Education and Empowerment	17
10	Chapter 10: Environmental Sustainability and Power	19
11	Chapter 11: The Ethics of Power	21
12	Chapter 12: The Path Forward	23
13	Chapter 13: Cultural Influence on Power	25
14	Chapter 14: Gender and Power Dynamics	27
15	Chapter 15: The Role of Technology in Social Change	29
16	Chapter 16: Power and Identity Politics	31
17	Chapter 17: The Role of Leadership in Shaping Power Dynamics	33

1

Chapter 1: The Origins of Power

Power, in its myriad forms, has been the cornerstone of civilization since the dawn of humanity. From ancient empires to modern states, the quest for power has driven wars, shaped societies, and fostered innovation. Understanding the origins of power requires a deep dive into the historical narratives that highlight the rise and fall of great leaders and empires. It is through this lens that we begin to appreciate the intrinsic value of power and its capacity to influence human behavior and societal structures.

In the ancient world, power was often wielded by monarchs and emperors who claimed divine right or lineage. These rulers established vast empires, often through conquest and coercion. The legitimacy of their rule was bolstered by elaborate rituals and symbolism that reinforced their supreme authority. This period saw the centralization of power in the hands of a few, who used it to control vast territories and diverse populations. The legacies of these rulers continue to echo through history, offering lessons on the nature of power and governance.

As societies evolved, so did the concept of power. The emergence of democratic principles in ancient Greece marked a significant shift in the power dynamic. Power began to be seen not just as a right of the elite but as a collective responsibility. This era introduced the idea of citizens having a voice in governance, paving the way for modern democratic systems. However, this transition was not without its challenges, as it often clashed with entrenched interests and traditional power structures.

The Renaissance and Enlightenment periods further transformed the understanding of power. Intellectual movements during these times challenged the established norms and advocated for reason, individualism, and scientific inquiry. This intellectual revolution laid the groundwork for political revolutions that sought to redistribute power more equitably. The American and French Revolutions, for instance, were pivotal in redefining the relationship between the state and its citizens, emphasizing liberty, equality, and fraternity as core values of modern governance.

2

Chapter 2: The Interplay of Politics and Power

Politics, at its core, is the practice of power. It is the means by which societies organize, govern, and make collective decisions. The interplay between politics and power is complex and multifaceted, often characterized by negotiation, compromise, and conflict. Political institutions, from parliaments to presidencies, are the arenas where power is exercised, contested, and legitimized. Understanding this interplay is crucial for appreciating the dynamics of modern governance and the challenges it faces.

Political power is often derived from various sources, including authority, charisma, and economic resources. Authority, whether derived from legal-rational systems or traditional customs, provides a legitimate basis for exercising power. Charismatic leaders, on the other hand, wield power through personal appeal and the ability to inspire and mobilize followers. Economic resources also play a crucial role in political power, as they provide the means to influence policy and decision-making processes.

The interaction between politics and power is also shaped by the distribution of power within society. In democratic systems, power is dispersed among various institutions and actors, creating a system of checks and balances. This dispersion is intended to prevent the concentration of power and ensure accountability. However, it also leads to complexities and inefficiencies in the decision-making process. In contrast, authoritarian systems centralize power in the hands of a single entity or group, often leading to more streamlined but less accountable governance.

The exercise of political power is not without its ethical considerations. The abuse of power for personal gain or to oppress others is a persistent issue in political systems. Corruption, nepotism, and authoritarianism are manifestations of such abuse. Ensuring ethical governance requires robust institutions, transparency, and active civic engagement. It is through these measures that societies can strive to create a political environment that is just, equitable, and responsive to the needs of its citizens.

3

Chapter 3: The Role of Society in Power Dynamics

Society is both the subject and object of power. It is within the fabric of society that power relations are established, contested, and perpetuated. Social structures, norms, and values play a critical role in shaping power dynamics. These societal elements influence who holds power, how it is exercised, and the extent to which it is accepted or resisted by the populace. Understanding the societal context is essential for analyzing power dynamics and their impact on social cohesion and stability.

Social institutions, such as the family, education, and religion, are fundamental in shaping individuals' perceptions of power. These institutions inculcate values, norms, and expectations that influence behavior and attitudes toward authority. For instance, the family unit often serves as the first arena where power dynamics are experienced and understood. Educational institutions further reinforce these dynamics by socializing individuals into the broader societal framework, while religious institutions provide moral and ethical guidance on the use and limits of power.

Civil society organizations play a crucial role in mediating power relations between the state and its citizens. These organizations, which include non-governmental organizations, advocacy groups, and community associations, provide a platform for collective action and social mobilization. They serve as a counterbalance to state power, advocating for the rights and interests of marginalized and vulnerable groups. By promoting social justice and accountability, civil society organizations contribute to a more balanced and inclusive power dynamic.

Social movements are another important aspect of societal power dynamics. These movements, often born out of perceived injustices and grievances, seek to challenge and transform existing power structures. Historical examples, such as the civil rights movement, the feminist movement, and the environmental movement, demonstrate the capacity of collective action to effect meaningful change. These movements highlight the potential of society to influence power relations and create a more equitable and just social order.

4

Chapter 4: Economic Power and Business Influence

Economic power is a fundamental aspect of the broader power equation, with business interests playing a significant role in shaping political and social landscapes. The influence of economic power can be seen in the ways businesses interact with governments, communities, and individuals. The pursuit of profit, innovation, and market dominance drives business activities, but it also raises questions about the ethical implications of corporate behavior and the concentration of wealth.

Large corporations often wield considerable power due to their economic resources and market influence. These corporations can shape public policy and regulatory frameworks through lobbying, political contributions, and partnerships with government agencies. The concentration of economic power in the hands of a few large entities raises concerns about market competition, consumer rights, and economic inequality. Ensuring fair and competitive markets requires robust regulatory frameworks and vigilant oversight to prevent abuses of power.

Small and medium-sized enterprises (SMEs) also play a critical role in the economic power dynamic. These businesses contribute to job creation, innovation, and local economic development. However, they often face challenges in competing with larger corporations and accessing resources. Supporting SMEs through favorable policies, access to finance, and capacity-building initiatives can help create a more balanced and inclusive economic landscape.

The ethical considerations of economic power are increasingly coming to the forefront of public discourse. Issues such as corporate social responsibility, environmental sustainability, and equitable labor practices are gaining prominence. Businesses are being called upon to consider the broader social and environmental impacts of their operations. By integrating ethical considerations into business practices, companies can contribute to a more sustainable and just economic system that benefits society as a whole.

5

Chapter 5: Globalization and the Shifting Power Dynamics

Globalization has significantly altered the landscape of power, creating new opportunities and challenges for political, social, and economic actors. The interconnectedness of global markets, the flow of information, and the movement of people have reshaped power dynamics on an international scale. Understanding the implications of globalization is crucial for navigating the complexities of modern governance and addressing the challenges it presents.

One of the key impacts of globalization is the diffusion of power across borders. Multinational corporations, international organizations, and transnational networks exert significant influence on global affairs. These actors operate across national boundaries, challenging traditional notions of sovereignty and state-centric power. The rise of global governance institutions, such as the United Nations and the World Trade Organization, reflects the need for coordinated responses to global issues, but it also raises questions about accountability and representation.

Globalization has also led to the emergence of new power centers in the global economy. Emerging markets and developing countries are playing an increasingly important role in shaping global economic trends. The rise of countries such as China, India, and Brazil as major economic powers is shifting the balance of power in the international system. This shift is accompanied by changes in geopolitical alliances, trade relationships, and global governance structures.

The social and cultural dimensions of globalization are equally significant. The spread of ideas, values, and cultural practices across borders has created a more interconnected and diverse global society. However, it has also led to tensions and conflicts as different cultures and values interact. Navigating these cultural dynamics requires an appreciation of diversity and a commitment to dialogue and understanding. By fostering intercultural exchange and cooperation, societies can harness the potential of globalization to create a more inclusive and harmonious world.

6

Chapter 6: Technology and the Future of Power

Technology is a driving force behind the evolution of power dynamics in the modern world. From the printing press to the internet, technological advancements have transformed the ways in which power is exercised, communicated, and contested. The digital age, in particular, has ushered in unprecedented changes in the realms of politics, society, and business. Understanding the implications of technological innovation is essential for anticipating future trends and addressing emerging technology.

The rise of social media platforms has revolutionized political communication and activism. These platforms provide a space for individuals and groups to share ideas, mobilize support, and challenge established power structures. Movements like the Arab Spring and the #MeToo campaign demonstrate the potential of technology to amplify voices and drive social change. However, the digital age also brings challenges such as misinformation, digital surveillance, and cyber-attacks, which pose significant risks to the integrity of political and social systems.

In the business world, technology has transformed how companies operate, compete, and interact with customers. The advent of e-commerce, big data, and artificial intelligence has created new business models and opportunities for innovation. Companies that leverage technology effectively can gain a competitive edge and drive growth. However, the rapid pace of technological change also raises concerns about job displacement, data privacy, and the ethical use of AI. Balancing innovation with ethical considerations is crucial for sustainable business practices.

Looking to the future, emerging technologies such as blockchain, quantum computing, and biotechnology hold the potential to further reshape power dynamics. These technologies promise to revolutionize industries, enhance security, and improve quality of life. However, they also raise complex ethical and regulatory questions. Ensuring that these technologies are developed and deployed responsibly requires collaboration between governments, businesses, and civil society. By fostering a culture of innovation and ethical stewardship, societies can harness the power of technology for the greater good.

7

Chapter 7: The Intersection of Business and Politics

The relationship between business and politics is deeply intertwined, with each influencing and shaping the other. Businesses often seek to influence political decisions and policies to create a favorable operating environment. This influence can be seen in various forms, such as lobbying, political donations, and public-private partnerships. Understanding the intersection of business and politics is crucial for analyzing the power dynamics that drive economic and political outcomes.

Lobbying is one of the primary mechanisms through which businesses exert political influence. By engaging with policymakers and government officials, businesses advocate for policies that align with their interests. While lobbying can promote constructive dialogue and informed decision-making, it also raises concerns about undue influence and unequal access to political power. Ensuring transparency and accountability in lobbying practices is essential for maintaining the integrity of democratic processes.

Political donations and campaign financing are other means by which businesses impact politics. Financial contributions to political campaigns can provide businesses with access to influential policymakers and decision-makers. However, the role of money in politics is a contentious issue, as it can lead to corruption and the erosion of public trust. Campaign finance reform and stringent regulations are necessary to mitigate the potential for undue influence and ensure a level playing field in the political arena.

Public-private partnerships (PPPs) represent a collaborative approach to addressing complex societal challenges. By leveraging the resources and expertise of both the public and private sectors, PPPs can drive innovation and deliver public goods and services more efficiently. Successful PPPs require clear frameworks, mutual accountability, and a shared commitment to public value. When implemented effectively, PPPs can enhance the effectiveness of governance and contribute to sustainable development.

8

Chapter 8: The Role of Media in Power Dynamics

The media plays a pivotal role in shaping power dynamics by influencing public opinion, holding power to account, and acting as a conduit for information. In democratic societies, a free and independent media is essential for ensuring transparency, accountability, and informed citizenry. The media's ability to investigate, report, and critique power structures makes it a crucial pillar of democracy and a vital check on the abuse of power.

The rise of digital media has transformed the landscape of journalism and information dissemination. Online platforms, social media, and citizen journalism have democratized access to information and expanded the diversity of voices in public discourse. However, the digital age also presents challenges such as the spread of misinformation, echo chambers, and the erosion of traditional journalistic standards. Navigating these challenges requires a commitment to media literacy, critical thinking, and ethical journalism.

Media ownership and concentration are significant factors that influence media power dynamics. A few large corporations often control major media outlets, raising concerns about editorial independence and diversity of perspectives. Ensuring media pluralism and preventing monopolistic practices are essential for maintaining a healthy and vibrant media ecosystem. Regulatory frameworks and public support for independent media can help safeguard the integrity and diversity of the media landscape.

The relationship between media and political power is complex and multifaceted. Media outlets can shape political narratives, influence election outcomes, and hold government officials accountable. However, media can also be susceptible to manipulation and propaganda, particularly in authoritarian regimes or conflict situations. Upholding media freedom and ensuring responsible journalism are critical for fostering democratic governance and protecting the public's right to know.

9

Chapter 9: Education and Empowerment

Education is a powerful tool for empowerment and a key driver of social and economic development. Access to quality education equips individuals with the knowledge, skills, and critical thinking abilities necessary to navigate and influence power dynamics. Education fosters a sense of agency and enables individuals to participate actively in political, social, and economic life. By promoting equality and inclusion, education contributes to the creation of more just and equitable societies.

The role of education in shaping power dynamics extends beyond formal schooling. Lifelong learning, vocational training, and informal education opportunities empower individuals to adapt to changing circumstances and pursue personal and professional growth. Education also plays a crucial role in challenging and transforming societal norms and stereotypes, promoting gender equality, and addressing issues of discrimination and marginalization.

Educational institutions serve as important arenas for the exchange of ideas and the cultivation of civic engagement. Universities, schools, and community centers provide spaces for critical inquiry, debate, and the development of social and political consciousness. By fostering a culture of dialogue and intellectual curiosity, educational institutions contribute to the formation of informed and active citizens who can engage constructively with power structures.

Ensuring equitable access to education is a fundamental challenge that requires concerted efforts from governments, civil society, and the private sector. Addressing barriers to education, such as poverty, discrimination, and geographic disparities, is essential for creating inclusive and resilient educational systems. By prioritizing education and investing in human capital, societies can harness the transformative power of education to drive progress and development.

10

Chapter 10: Environmental Sustainability and Power

Environmental sustainability is an increasingly important aspect of the power equation, as the global community grapples with the challenges of climate change, resource depletion, and ecological degradation. The quest for sustainable development requires a rethinking of how power is exercised and distributed, with a focus on balancing economic growth, social well-being, and environmental stewardship. Understanding the interplay between environmental sustainability and power is crucial for addressing the pressing environmental issues of our time.

Governments, businesses, and civil society play key roles in promoting environmental sustainability. Governments can enact policies and regulations that incentivize sustainable practices and penalize environmental harm. Businesses can adopt sustainable business models, invest in green technologies, and engage in corporate social responsibility initiatives. Civil society organizations can advocate for environmental justice, raise awareness, and mobilize communities to take action. Collaborative efforts across these sectors are essential for achieving meaningful progress toward sustainability.

The transition to a sustainable economy requires addressing the power dynamics that drive environmental exploitation and inequality. Wealthy nations and corporations often have a disproportionate impact on the environment, while marginalized communities and developing countries bear the brunt of environmental degradation. Ensuring a just transition involves redistributing power and resources to support vulnerable populations and promote equitable access to the benefits of sustainability.

Innovative solutions and technologies hold great promise for advancing environmental sustainability. Renewable energy, circular economy practices, and sustainable agriculture are among the approaches that can reduce environmental impact and enhance resilience. However, the adoption of these solutions requires supportive policies, investment, and a commitment to long-term sustainability goals. By embracing innovation and collaboration, societies can create a more sustainable and equitable future for all.

11

Chapter 11: The Ethics of Power

The exercise of power is inherently linked to ethical considerations, as it involves decisions that impact the lives and well-being of individuals and communities. Ethical leadership and governance are essential for ensuring that power is used responsibly and for the greater good. Understanding the ethical dimensions of power requires a commitment to principles such as justice, transparency, accountability, and respect for human rights.

Ethical dilemmas often arise in the context of power, as leaders and decision-makers navigate complex and competing interests. Balancing the needs of different stakeholders, addressing conflicts of interest, and making decisions with long-term consequences require a strong ethical foundation. Ethical decision-making involves considering the broader impact of actions, being guided by moral values, and prioritizing the welfare of society as a whole.

Transparency and accountability are critical components of ethical power. Open and transparent decision-making processes build trust and legitimacy, while accountability mechanisms ensure that power is exercised in a responsible and just manner. Corruption, abuse of power, and lack of accountability undermine the ethical use of power and erode public trust.

Strengthening transparency and accountability requires robust institutions, legal frameworks, and active civic participation.

Fostering a culture of ethical leadership involves education, training, and the promotion of ethical standards across all levels of society. Ethical leadership should be modeled by individuals in positions of authority and reinforced through organizational policies and practices. By prioritizing ethics in the exercise of power, societies can create an environment that promotes fairness, justice, and the well-being of all citizens.

12

Chapter 12: The Path Forward

The power equation is a dynamic and evolving concept, shaped by the interplay of politics, society, and business. As we look to the future, it is essential to consider the lessons learned from the intersections of politics, society, and business. The complexities of power dynamics require a holistic approach that acknowledges the interconnectedness of these domains. As we navigate the challenges and opportunities of the 21st century, it is crucial to foster a collaborative, inclusive, and ethical framework for exercising power. This approach can help create a more just, equitable, and sustainable world for future generations.

Building a resilient and adaptable society involves embracing innovation, promoting education, and prioritizing sustainability. Innovation drives progress and addresses pressing global issues, while education empowers individuals and fosters a culture of informed citizenship. Sustainability ensures that development meets the needs of the present without compromising the ability of future generations to meet their own needs. By integrating these principles into the power equation, societies can create a balanced and forward-looking approach to governance and development.

Collaboration and dialogue are essential for addressing the complex and interrelated challenges of our time. Governments, businesses, civil society, and individuals must work together to create solutions that reflect diverse perspectives and address the root causes of social, economic, and environmental issues. By fostering a culture of cooperation and mutual respect, we can build bridges across divides and create a more cohesive and inclusive global community.

Ultimately, the path forward requires a commitment to ethical leadership, transparency, and accountability. By prioritizing these values, societies can ensure that power is exercised responsibly and for the benefit of all. The power equation is not static; it is shaped by the actions and decisions of individuals and institutions. By striving for a just and equitable distribution of power, we can create a world where politics, society, and business work together harmoniously to achieve common goals and advance the well-being of all people.

13

Chapter 13: Cultural Influence on Power

Culture plays an integral role in shaping power dynamics within any society. Cultural norms, values, and traditions inform what is considered legitimate authority, acceptable behavior, and justifiable action. These cultural elements influence the ways in which power is acquired, maintained, and exercised. Understanding the cultural context is crucial for analyzing how power is perceived and enacted within different communities.

In many societies, cultural heritage and historical narratives are deeply intertwined with concepts of power. Myths, legends, and historical events often serve as sources of identity and legitimacy for leaders and institutions. For example, national heroes and foundational myths can be used to galvanize public support and reinforce the authority of the state. The role of cultural symbolism in power dynamics highlights the importance of narrative and meaning in the exercise of power.

Cultural diversity presents both opportunities and challenges for power dynamics. In multicultural societies, power must be negotiated and shared among different cultural groups, each with its own distinct values and perspectives. This diversity can enrich the social fabric and foster innovation, but it can also lead to tensions and conflicts. Promoting intercultural dialogue and mutual respect is essential for creating a harmonious and inclusive society.

Globalization has accelerated the exchange of cultural practices and ideas, leading to a more interconnected world. This cultural intermingling can reshape power dynamics by introducing new norms and values that challenge traditional power structures. The global spread of democratic ideals, human rights, and consumer culture exemplifies how cultural influence transcends national boundaries and reshapes the global power equation.

14

Chapter 14: Gender and Power Dynamics

Gender is a critical factor in the analysis of power dynamics. Historically, power has been predominantly held by men, leading to systemic gender inequalities that persist to this day. Understanding the role of gender in power dynamics requires an examination of both the overt and subtle ways in which gender influences access to power, representation, and decision-making.

The feminist movement has been instrumental in challenging gender-based power imbalances and advocating for greater gender equality. Through activism, policy advocacy, and education, feminists have sought to dismantle patriarchal structures and promote women's empowerment. This movement has led to significant strides in women's rights, including greater political representation, reproductive rights, and workplace equality.

Despite progress, gender disparities remain pervasive in many areas, including politics, business, and society. Women often face barriers to leadership positions, unequal pay, and gender-based violence. Addressing these disparities requires targeted policies, cultural change, and ongoing advocacy efforts. By promoting gender equality, societies can create more inclusive and equitable power dynamics that benefit all individuals.

The intersectionality of gender with other social categories, such as race, class, and sexuality, further complicates power dynamics. Women of color, LGBTQ+ individuals, and those from marginalized communities often experience compounded discrimination and exclusion. Recognizing and addressing these intersecting forms of oppression is essential for achieving true gender equality and fostering a more just and inclusive society.

15

Chapter 15: The Role of Technology in Social Change

Technology has been a catalyst for social change throughout history, from the invention of the printing press to the rise of the internet. Technological advancements have transformed how societies communicate, organize, and mobilize. By enabling new forms of social interaction and collective action, technology has the potential to reshape power dynamics and drive social progress.

The internet and social media have revolutionized the way information is disseminated and consumed. These platforms have democratized access to information, allowing individuals to share their voices and connect with others on a global scale. Movements like Black Lives Matter and Fridays for Future demonstrate the power of technology to amplify marginalized voices and mobilize collective action for social justice.

While technology can empower individuals and communities, it also presents challenges and risks. The spread of misinformation, digital surveillance, and cyber harassment are significant concerns in the digital age. Ensuring that technology is used ethically and responsibly requires robust regulatory frameworks, digital literacy education, and a commitment to protecting individual rights and freedoms.

Emerging technologies, such as artificial intelligence and blockchain, hold promise for furthering social change. These technologies have the potential to enhance transparency, improve access to services, and address systemic inequalities. However, their impact will depend on how they are developed and implemented. By prioritizing ethical considerations and inclusivity, societies can harness the transformative power of technology for the greater good.

16

Chapter 16: Power and Identity Politics

Identity politics refers to the ways in which individuals and groups mobilize around shared aspects of their identity, such as race, ethnicity, gender, or sexual orientation, to advance their interests and challenge systemic oppression. Identity politics plays a significant role in shaping power dynamics by highlighting the diverse experiences and perspectives of marginalized communities.

The civil rights movement, LGBTQ+ rights movement, and indigenous rights movement are examples of how identity politics has been used to challenge and transform power structures. These movements have raised awareness of systemic injustices and advocated for policies that promote equality and inclusion. By centering the experiences of marginalized communities, identity politics seeks to create a more equitable and just society.

Critics of identity politics argue that it can lead to division and polarization by emphasizing differences rather than commonalities. However, proponents assert that recognizing and addressing the unique challenges faced by marginalized groups is essential for achieving true equality. Balancing the need for unity with the imperative of addressing specific forms of oppression is a key challenge in contemporary power dynamics.

Identity politics also intersects with other forms of political activism, such as economic justice and environmental sustainability. Understanding the interconnectedness of these issues is crucial for building coalitions and creating comprehensive strategies for social change. By embracing the diversity of experiences and perspectives within society, identity politics can contribute to a more inclusive and holistic approach to power and governance.

17

Chapter 17: The Role of Leadership in Shaping Power Dynamics

Leadership is a central element in the exercise and distribution of power. Effective leadership involves the ability to inspire, mobilize, and guide others toward a common goal. The qualities and styles of leaders can significantly influence power dynamics within organizations, communities, and societies.

Different leadership styles, such as transformational, transactional, and servant leadership, offer various approaches to wielding power. Transformational leaders seek to inspire and empower followers through vision and charisma, while transactional leaders focus on achieving specific goals through rewards and incentives. Servant leaders prioritize the needs of their followers and emphasize ethical and inclusive leadership. Each style has its strengths and weaknesses, and the most effective leaders often adapt their approach to the context and needs of their constituents.

The ethical considerations of leadership are paramount in shaping power dynamics. Leaders have a responsibility to use their power for the greater good, uphold principles of justice and fairness, and act with integrity.

Ethical leadership builds trust and legitimacy, fostering a positive and inclusive environment. Conversely, unethical leadership, characterized by corruption, abuse of power, and self-interest, undermines trust and perpetuates inequality.

Leadership is not confined to formal positions of authority; it can emerge from any level of society. Grassroots leaders, community organizers, and activists play vital roles in challenging power structures and driving social change. By cultivating and supporting diverse forms of leadership, societies can create more resilient and adaptive power dynamics that reflect the needs and aspirations of all individuals.

Book Description

"The Power Equation: Where Politics, Society, and Business Collide":

In "**The Power Equation: Where Politics, Society, and Business Collide**," we delve into the intricate relationships that define our modern world. This compelling exploration reveals how politics, society, and business intersect to shape power dynamics in profound ways. From the historical origins of power to the contemporary challenges of globalization and technology, this book provides a comprehensive analysis of the forces that drive change and influence human behavior.

Through twelve insightful chapters, readers will journey through the evolution of political power, the role of social institutions, and the impact of economic influence. The narrative highlights the significance of cultural and gender dynamics, the power of education, and the ethical considerations that underpin responsible governance. With a keen focus on the future, the book also examines emerging technologies, environmental sustainability, and the shifting balance of global power.

"**The Power Equation**" is an essential read for anyone seeking to understand the complex interplay of forces that shape our world. Whether you're a student of politics, a business leader, or a curious mind, this book offers valuable insights and thought-provoking perspectives on the power dynamics that define our lives.

www.ingramcontent.com/pod-product-compliance
Lightning Source LLC
LaVergne TN
LVHW010442070526
838199LV00066B/6138